My Hero's Journey

Plotting your book from start to finish

A Journal

Name of your book

Series number

PATTI ROBERTS

Copyright © 2017 Patti Roberts
All rights reserved.

ISBN-13: 978-1974277520

ISBN-10: 1974277526

A NOTE TO THE WRITER

If you are anything like me, you have notes and note pads scattered everywhere. Originally, I created this journal for myself as a go to manual for future books, but after seeing how helpful and time-saving it was for keeping track of my stories and characters neatly in one place, I decided to share it with other writers embarking on their writing journey.

What you'll need:
A great story idea. Great characters.
Pencil and an eraser - I highly recommend using a pencil, allowing you to make changes when necessary.

I look forward to you contacting me on the completion of your book. Good luck and happy writing. Patti Roberts. pattiroberts7@gmail.com

CONTENTS

There are two sections to this journal.
The first section is designed to help you plot your story and list character profiles to keep you on track. Your blueprint, if you like.

What is the Hero's Journey? Three main acts.
Blank pages for you to plot your story.
Your characters. Who are they?
In this section, add notes and pictures for future reference.
The Hero's Journey explained.

The second section of this journal explains the Hero's Journey in chapter form, guiding you through each stage from start to finish. Includes examples from movies and books.

Chapter 1	Ordinary world	1
Chapter 2	Call to adventure	3
Chapter 3	Refusal of the call	5
Chapter 4	Meeting the mentor	7
Chapter 5	Crossing the threshold	9
Chapter 6	Tests, allies & enemies	11
Chapter 7	Approach	13
Chapter 8	Supreme ordeal	15
Chapter 9	Reward	17
Chapter 10	The road back	19
Chapter 11	Resurrection	21
Chapter 12	Return with the treasure	23

The Hero's Journey diagram	25
The Hero's inner Journey diagram	26
The next book in the series	27
About the author	38
References	42

WHAT IS THE HERO'S JOURNEY?

The Hero's Journey is an archetype that forms the building blocks of most modern movies, books, and TV shows. The Hero's Journey formula works for stories that are character-driven, focusing on overcoming obstacles while experiencing fundamental change as the story progresses. It takes the protagonist from the mundane "Ordinary World" we can all identify with in some way to an unknown "Special World" where the hero must face challenges and overcome obstacles, both externally and internally.

THERE ARE 3 MAIN ACTS IN THE 12 STAGES:

ACT 1
1. The ordinary world
2. The call to adventure
3. Refusal of the call
4. Meeting with the mentor
5. Crossing the threshold into the Special World

ACT 2
6. Tests, allies, and enemies
7. Approach to the innermost cave
8. The ordeal
9. Reward

ACT 3
10. The road back
11. The resurrection
12. Return with the treasure

OUTLINE YOUR STORY USING THE HERO'S JOURNEY

Stage 1- The Ordinary World

Who is your hero? Describe their mundane life.

Stage 2 - The Call to Adventure

What is the central conflict that needs solving in your story?

Stage 3 - Refusal Of The Call

How do you anticipate your hero reacting to the problem?

Stage 4 - Meeting With The Mentor

Who is the mentor guiding your hero through the resolution of their problem?

Stage 5 - Crossing the First Threshold

Once your hero trusts the mentor, they will be on board to hear their guidance and put their tips into action.

Stage 6 - Tests, Allies, and Enemies

Introduce your hero to the tools, resources, training and experts they need to become acquainted with to solve their problem. This is also the point in the story where you advise them what not to do.

Stage 7 - Approach to the Innermost Cave

Once your hero learns he has a general idea of what's happening, it is time to put their solution to the problem into action.

Stage 8 - The Ordeal

Your hero will have to test their knowledge and skills they have learned in some way.

Stage 9 - The Reward

Having succeeded at their first task, the hero will experience the rewards of their efforts. But their journey isn't over yet.

Stage 10 - The Road Back

It's important that the hero understands that the problem is not solved yet.

Stage 11 - The Resurrection

At this stage in the story, your hero should know how to address the ongoing problem and how to overcome it.

Stage 12 - Return with the treasure

Your hero emerged from his adventure wiser and equipped with the knowledge and skills to face the same or similar problems in the future.

LIST YOUR CHARACTERS. WHO ARE THEY?

Know your characters, particularly your main characters. List their characteristics. Height, weight, eye, and hair color, abilities, fears, hopes, and dreams. Birthday, favorite color, clothes. Do they have abilities?

You may not use all of this information in your story, but it will help you know your characters and be more consistent with who they are.

I like to choose an actor to represent each of my main characters – my dream team if you like. I pin pictures of my characters on cork boards near my writing desk, but if you choose to do your writing in random locations, such as cafes, pasting pictures of your characters in this journal will allow you to take them with you.

The Eight Character Archetypes of the Hero's Journey

1. Hero
2. Mentor
3. Ally
4. Herald
5. Trickster
6. Shapeshifter
7. Guardian
8. Shadow

Add your character's names, pictures and anything else of importance on the following pages.

The hero.

The hero is the tour guide in the adventure that is your story. It's critical that the audience can relate to them because they will experience the story through their eyes. During the journey, the hero will leave the ordinary world they are familiar with and enter a new one. This new world will be so different that whatever skills the hero used previously will no longer be sufficient. Together, the hero and the audience will master the rules of the new world and ultimately save the day.

Examples: Katniss Everdeen from The Hunger Games, Beatrice Prior from Divergent, and Luke Skywalker from Star Wars.

The mentor.

The hero has to learn how to survive in the new world relatively fast, so the mentor appears early on to offer them guidance and skills. This mentor will describe how the new world operates and instruct the hero in using any abilities they might already possess.

Example: Haymitch Abernathy from the Hunger Games, Dumbledore from Harry Potter, and Mr. Miyagi from the Karate Kid.

The ally.

The hero will have some huge challenges ahead; too great for one person to face alone. They'll need someone to distract the guards, hack into the mainframe, or carry their gear. Often a best friend – a sidekick.

Examples: Robin from Batman, Ron and Hermione from Harry Potter, and Sam Gamgee from Lord of the Rings.

The herald.

The herald appears near the beginning to announce the need for change in the hero's life. They are the catalyst that sets the whole adventure in motion. While they often bring news of a threat, they can also simply show a dissatisfied hero a tempting glimpse into a new life. Occasionally they single the hero out, picking them for a journey they wouldn't otherwise take. The herald need not be a person - a message on a scrap of paper, letters, an invitation, or a radio broadcast can serve equally to trigger change.

Examples: Effie from the Hunger Games, R2D2 from Star Wars, and the letters from Harry Potter.

The trickster.

The trickster adds fun and comic relief to the story. When times are gloomy or emotionally tense, the trickster gives the audience a welcomed break. A good trickster offers an outside perspective and asks the important questions. They may be a character who keeps changing sides or whose allegiance is uncertain.

Examples: Dobby from Harry Potter, Merry and Pippin from Lord of the Rings, and C3PO from Star Wars.

The shapeshifter.

The shapeshifter blurs the line between ally and enemy. Often they begin as an ally, then betray the hero at a critical moment. Other times, their loyalty is in question as they waver back and forth. They provide a tantalizing combination of appeal and possible danger. Shapeshifters benefit stories by creating interesting relationships among the characters. The Shapeshifter helps show the character's inner conflict or unease about certain situations.

Examples: Gollum from Lord of the Rings, The wolves from Twilight, and Gilderoy Lockhart from Harry Potter.

The Guardian.

The guardian, or threshold guardian as they are sometimes called, tests the hero before they face their challenges. They can appear at any stage in your story, but they always block an entrance or border of some kind. The job of the guardian is to get the hero to rethink whether or not he wishes to proceed on this adventure. Then the hero must prove their worth by answering a question/riddle, sneaking past, or defeating the guardian in combat.
Examples: Obi-Wan from Star Wars, Glinda from the Wizard of Oz, and Peter and Eric from Divergent.

The Shadow.

Shadows are the villains in your story. They exist to create threat and conflict and to give the hero something to struggle/fight against. Most shadows do not see themselves as villains, but merely as heroes in their own beliefs. The shadow shows the audience the twisted person the hero could become if they head down the wrong path, and highlights the hero's inner struggle.
Examples: Voldemort from Harry Potter, Sauron from Lord of the Rings, and Maleficent from Sleeping Beauty.

1 ORDINARY WORLD

ACT 1

- The ordinary world
- The call to adventure
- Refusal of the call
- Meeting with the mentor
- Crossing the threshold into the Special World

The hero is introduced sympathetically so the reader can identify with the situation or dilemma. Introduce your hero in their everyday environment with some personal history. Create a situation in the hero's life which is pulling them in different directions and causing stress.

Most epic stories ultimately take us to a world entirely different to our own, so create a world foreign to the hero in your story. If you're telling a story about a character out of his customary element, you need to create a contrast by showing him in his boring, ordinary world first.

In Star Wars you see Luke Skywalker being bored to death as a farm boy before his adventure begins.

YOUR NOTES:

2 THE CALL TO ADVENTURE

Something shakes up the situation in the story, either from external pressures or from something rising up in the hero, forcing him to face the changes happening around him.

The hero is presented with a problem, challenge, or adventure that takes him out of his comfort zone.

In a detective story, it's the hero being assigned a new case/mystery to solve. In a romantic comedy, it could be the first sight of a new love interest. Perhaps they hit if off straight away, or start off as opponents, rivals or enemies?

In Star Wars, it's Princess Leia's holographic message to Obi-Wan Kenobi, bringing Luke into the adventure that will change his life forever.

YOUR NOTES:

3 REFUSAL OF THE CALL

Often at this point, the hero pulls back from the adventure. The hero is facing the greatest of all fears – fear of the unknown and is hesitant in moving forward.

The hero soon becomes overwhelmed however and turns away from the adventure. After a time he soon picks himself up and returns to the adventure. At this point, another character may express the uncertainty and danger ahead.

For example, at this point Luke refuses Obi-Wan's call to adventure, and returns to the safety of his aunt and uncle's farmhouse, only to find they've been murdered by the Emperor's stormtroopers. Motivated by anger and revenge, Luke is no longer reluctant and is eager to participate in the adventure.

YOUR NOTES:

4 MEETING WITH THE MENTOR

By this stage, you will also have to introduce a character who is the hero's mentor/mentors. The mentor gives advice and sometimes magical powers/weapons.

The mentor will assist the hero for a time. Eventually, though, the hero must face the unknown by himself. Sometimes the Wise Old Man/Woman is required to give the hero a push to get him motivated once again.

This mentor may give the hero training, equipment or advice that will help him continue his journey.

In Star Wars, this is when Obi-Wan give's Luke his father's light saber.

YOUR NOTES:

5 CROSSING THE THRESHOLD

The hero enters the Special World of the story for the first time at this point. This is the moment when the story takes off, and the adventure really picks up the pace.

In a romantic novel, this is when the romance begins, the fireworks moment.

There is no turning back. The hero is now committed to his journey, leaving his old life behind and enters the new phase of his life clouded with unfamiliar rules and values.

YOUR NOTES:

6 TESTS, ALLIES, ENEMIES

- Tests, allies, and enemies
- Approach to the innermost cave
- The ordeal
- Reward

The Special World. At this point, the hero is forced to make allies and enemies in the adventure and has to pass certain tests and challenges that are part of his training.

The hero learns the rules of his new world. During this time he meets friends and comes face to face with foes.

YOUR NOTES:

7 APPROACH

Setbacks occur, sometimes causing the hero to try a new approach or adopt new ideas. The hero comes at last to a dangerous place, where the object of the quest up to this point was hidden.

Here, the hero is faced with danger to save a loved one, or in a battle to gain a treasure or something or someone of importance. Sometimes it's just the hero confronting and overcoming fears.

The hero and newfound allies prepare for a major challenge in the adventure.

YOUR NOTES:

8 THE SUPREME ORDEAL

Near the middle of the story, the hero enters a central space in the Special World and confronts death or faces his or her greatest fear.

This is the moment in the story when the hero reaches rock bottom. This part is a critical moment in any story, an ordeal in which the hero appears that he is going to die. It's a dark time for the character.

In Star Wars, the group rescues Princess Leia, Luke nearly drowns in the sewage system, and Darth Vadar kills Obi-Wan Kenobi.

YOUR NOTES:

9 REWARD

Having just escaped death in the previous chapter, the hero now takes possession of the treasure he's been seeking throughout the story.

The hero may also win his prize, in some cases the woman he loves. The hero's supreme ordeal may grant him a better understanding of a situation, leading to reconciliation.

The hero takes possession of the treasure won by facing death. There may be a celebration, but there is also the danger of losing the treasure again.

In Star Wars, Luke joins the rebels to destroy the Death Star.

YOUR NOTES:

10 THE ROAD BACK

- The road back
- The resurrection
- Return with the treasure

The hero's not out of the woods quite yet, however. About three-fourths of the way through the story, the hero is driven to complete the adventure, leaving the Special World to ensure the treasure is safe and taken home. Often a chase scene signals the urgency and danger of the mission.

In Star Wars, Luke chooses to remain in the battle with his friends and take down the Galactic Empire.

YOUR NOTES:

11 RESURRECTION.

At the climax of the story, the hero is severely tested once more on the threshold of going home. He is victorious in a last sacrifice, another moment of death and rebirth.

The hero emerges from the Special World, transformed by his experience.

In Star Wars, Luke uses his power of the Force to destroy the Death Star.

By the hero's action, the divisions that were in conflict at the beginning are finally resolved.

YOUR NOTES:

12 RETURN WITH THE TREASURE

The hero has come full circle, back to his ordinary world, but the adventure wouldn't be complete unless he brought back the treasure or learned some lesson from the Special World. Sometimes it's knowledge or experience, but unless he comes back with the treasure or some win for mankind, he's doomed to repeat the adventure until he does.

Sometimes the treasure is a loved one or just the knowledge that the Special World exists and can be survived, and sometimes it's just coming home with a story to tell about an incredible adventure.

In Star Wars, Luke wins a medal and takes his first steps towards becoming a Jedi.

Examples of books/movies using the Hero's Journey:
Star Wars.
Lord of the Rings.
Never Ending Story.
The wizard of Oz.
Harry Potter.
MATRIX.
Divergent.
Hunger Games.

YOUR NOTES:

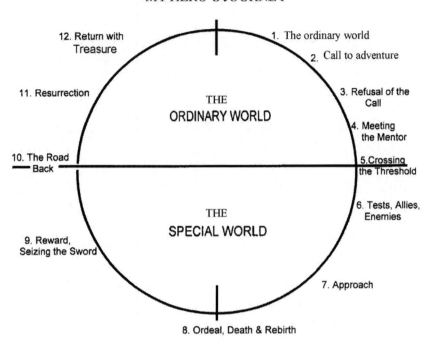

MY HERO'S INNER JOURNEY

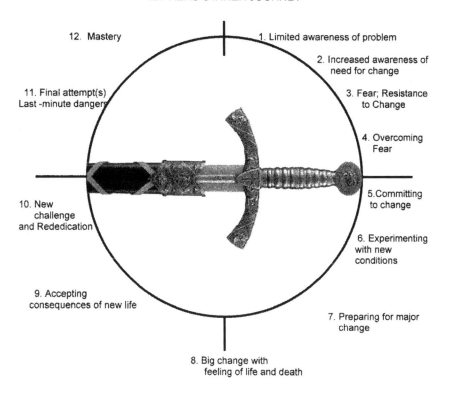

1. Limited awareness of problem
2. Increased awareness of need for change
3. Fear; Resistance to Change
4. Overcoming Fear
5. Committing to change
6. Experimenting with new conditions
7. Preparing for major change
8. Big change with feeling of life and death
9. Accepting consequences of new life
10. New challenge and Rededication
11. Final attempt(s) Last-minute dangers
12. Mastery

THE NEXT BOOK IN THE SERIES

If you are writing a series, jot down ideas for the next book/books. You may need to answer questions from the previous book or tie up loose ends.

ABOUT THE AUTHOR

PATTI ROBERTS was born in Brisbane Australia but soon moved to Darwin in the Northern Territory. Her son Luke was born in 1980. Her son and grandson are the two leading men in Patti's life. She currently lives in Cairns, Queensland, where she is writing the Paradox series of books. Since then, Patti has commenced writing the Witchwood Estate series, and written a contemporary romance, About Three Authors – Whoever Said Love Was Easy? Patti has also published a non-fiction book, Surviving Tracy, featuring true stories from survivors of Cyclone Tracy which devastated Darwin in the Northern Territory in 1974.

Future books to look out for:
KLA2EEN – First Contact, a sci-fi series. We are not alone in the universe.
I'm That Girl. Contemporary drama/romance.
Girl Returned – a standalone sci-fi novel about alien abduction.

In her spare time, Patti designs book covers and formats for authors.

CONTACT

Email: pattiroberts7@gmail.com
Facebook: https://www.facebook.com/PattiParadox
Twitter: twitter.com/PattiRoberts7
Goodreads: https://www.goodreads.com/author/show/980856.Patti_Roberts
Newsletter: http://bit.ly/PattiRobertsNewsletter

Publications by Patti Roberts

Freebies.

Once Were Friends.
A 20k prologue to Whoever Said Love Was Easy?

Witchwood Estate collectables - The Witches' Journal – book 1.

A collection of recipes, poetry, Witches' pantry, tea leaves, broom history, familiars, candles, flowers, and more.

Diffusing Essential Oils.

Writing Tips From Authors.

Believe.

Witchwood Estate – Going Home – (book 1) FREE

Paradox – The Angels Are Here (book 1) FREE

Witchwood Estate

Witchwood Estate – Going Home – (book 1) FREE

Witchwood Estate – Ferntree Falls

Witchwood Estate – Print Edition (book 1 and 2)

Witchwood Estate – Cursed (book 3)

Witchwood Estate – Timeless (book 4)

Witchwood Estate – Witches Bitches (book 5)

Paradox Series

Paradox – The Angels Are Here (book 1) 2010 FREE

Paradox – Progeny Of Innocence (book 2)

Paradox – Bound By Blood (book 3)

Paradox – Equilibrium (book 4)

Paradox – Elemental (book 5)

Standalone Novel

About Three Authors – Whoever Said Love Was Easy?

Non-fiction novel

Surviving Tracy – true stories from the survivors of Cyclone Tracy.

Reference.

MLA: "New Campers: A Hero's Journey - Summer Camp Programming.". N.p., n.d. Web. 10 Aug. 2017 <http://www.summercamppro.com/new-campers-a-heros-journey/>.

MLA: "Plotting Is Fun! How To Keep Your Story From Getting Hung ..." N.p., n.d. Web. 10 Aug. 2017 <http://slideplayer.com/slide/8767309/>.

MLA: "The Eight Character Archetypes Of The Hero's Journey ..." N.p., n.d. Web. 10 Aug. 2017 <https://mythcreants.com/blog/the-eight-character-archetypes-of-the-heros-journey/>.

MLA: "Creative Writing - Hero Story Unit Flashcards | Quizlet." N.p., n.d. Web. 10 Aug. 2017 <https://quizlet.com/182266014/creative-writing-hero-story-unit-flash-cards/>.

MLA: "A Practical Guide To The Hero With A Thousand Faces By ..." N.p., n.d. Web. 10 Aug. 2017 <http://skepticfiles.org/atheist2/hero.htm>.

MLA: "Creative Writing - Hero Story Unit Flashcards | Quizlet." N.p., n.d. Web. 10 Aug. 2017 <https://quizlet.com/182266014/creative-writing-hero-story-unit-flash-cards/>.

MLA: "Hero's Journey Outline - The Writer's Journey." N.p., n.d. Web. 10 Aug. 2017 \<http://www.thewritersjourney.com/hero's_journey.htm>.

MLA: "The Hero's Journey Flash Cards Flashcards | Quizlet." N.p., n.d. Web. 10 Aug. 2017 <https://quizlet.com/81154218/the-heros-journey-flash-cards-flash-cards/>.

MLA: "Created In Partnership With The Educational Team." N.p., n.d. Web. 10 Aug. 2017 <http://cdnvideo.dolimg.com/cdn_assets/fcc5b86eec81c5d934e5ca5e96055cea87cae402.p>.

MLA: "Common In Hero Films - Star Wars, Harry Potter, Lotr ..." N.p., n.d. Web. 10 Aug. 2017 <http://socialvani.com/hero-star-wars-harry-potter-lotr-matrix-spiderman-lion-kin>.

Made in the USA
Middletown, DE
11 December 2018